THE
CANADIAN
GARDENER'S
JOURNAL

THE

CANADIAN

GARDENER'S

JOURNAL

BRIAN BIXLEY

KEY PORTER BOOKS

Frontispiece:

Colchicums in September.

The following publisher has given permission
to use quoted material: From ''The Midsum-
mer Garden'' in *Collected Poems* by Miriam
Waddington. Copyright © 1986 by Miriam
Waddington. Reprinted by permission of
Oxford University Press.

Canadian Cataloguing in Publication Data

Bixley, Brian
    The Canadian gardener's journal

ISBN 1-55013-270-9

1. Gardening — Canada — Miscellanea.
I. Title.

SB453.3.C3B58   1991   635'.0971
C90-095349-7

Design: Scott Richardson
Illustrations: Andrew Woodhouse
Map: Jim Loates
Typesetting: Compeer Typographic Services
Limited
Printed and bound in Canada

Key Porter Books Limited
70 The Esplanade
Toronto, Ontario
Canada M5E 1R2

91   92   93   94   95   5   4   3   2   1

For Maureen, who makes everything possible

Introduction

The gardener's year varies so much from east to west, north to south, that it is not possible to provide in a few pages any kind of comprehensive guide to gardening for all regions of North America. When the snowdrops are flowering in Victoria, Ontario's gardens are likely to be covered with snow. Differences in rainfall, temperatures, humidity, soil conditions and snow cover mean that gardening possibilities vary widely across the continent. In this journal, the reader will find some hints and suggestions about plants, garden design and useful techniques derived from my own experience or from my reading of garden literature or simply from my listening carefully to the wise words that gardeners across the continent have to say to one another.

Included are plant portraits of some members of the same *genus* (*Narcissus*, *Tulipa*), or sometimes of a group of associated plants (small trees, annuals). I have usually written about plants with which I am familiar from our own garden in Zone 3. Since most of North America gardens in gentler conditions than the ones we experience, anything we can grow can probably, with some care and attention to special requirements, be grown elsewhere.

Steps lead to yet another vantage point from which to view the garden.

Though I have included a zone hardiness map at the back of the book, and have sometimes quoted the orthodox hardiness ratings, do not be discouraged by them from trying plants that apparently will not be hardy. When I began gardening, people were always saying, most amiably, that such-and-such a plant could not be grown in our region, and it took me quite a long time to realize that, in many cases, they hadn't actually tried to grow the plant, but were simply quoting someone else. Even if the plant had not thrived for them, that didn't mean that it wouldn't do perfectly well somewhere else nearby.

The concept of microclimates is almost as fashionable as mulches and ornamental grasses, but vastly more important, and it is crucial to realize that you may do well with a plant that behaves quite miserably in a neighbor's garden because you are able to give it some special situation or care. There are all kinds of plants growing in our garden that are "not hardy," and there are quite a few plants that the books assure us should be problem-free but that we are unable to grow well.

A open gateway invites one into the garden beyond.

At the end of the book is space for recording jobs done, to serve to remind you *next* year of what you should be doing now. Also included is space for recording jobs that should have been done, which you can fill in later as you wake up with a guilty start. All of us forget or overlook tasks that would have been better done *last* week, and noting them here will enable you to build up a schedule that is appropriate for your garden, and that may include such pleasures as a reminder that last week was when you should have gone to look for morels on the edge of the woods at the end of your road.

This space will help you to organize your jobs according to the size of your garden, its needs, the time you have available for it, the dates of your first and last frosts, whether or not you have reliable snow cover and so on. If you keep these notes regularly, you will gradually become your own best expert. In this sense, the journal is truly a perennial one, for it will grow in usefulness year by year.

Dalmatian Bellflower (*Campanula portenschlagiana*).

January

Your chances of gardening success will increase if you know what type of soil you have in your garden. The mineral content of topsoil is likely to reflect the qualities of the rock below, but not always; it may have been pushed there by glaciers or washed there by rivers. This means that a guess may lead you in the wrong direction. Call your provincial ministry of agriculture to see if you can obtain a soil map and to find out if they provide analysis of soil samples.

1

NEW YEAR'S DAY

2

3

4

5

6

The winter garden and birds at the feeder.

7

A small greenhouse filled with choice plants.

8

9

10

11

12

13

14

15

Musk Mallow
(*Malva moschata*).

All plants have a scientific botanical name that is intended to identify the plant precisely. Most of us, when we begin gardening, get along quite happily without knowing these names, though in many cases — *Forsythia*, *Hydrangea*, *Dahlia*, *Zinnia*, for example — we are using part of the botanical name without knowing that we are doing so.

The botanical name is called a "binomial," because it is divided into two parts. The first is the generic name or "genus"; the names I gave above are all genera (the plural of genus). This is followed by a specific name, which usually describes some aspect of the plant, e.g., *Hydrangea quercifolia*, where "folia" refers to the foliage, and "querc" refers to *Quercus*, which is itself the generic name for oak. So we know that it is the "oak-leaved hydrangea" that is being described. All genera contain at least one species, and all the species within a genus have some botanical characteristics in common.

"I can endure no plants in pots — a plant in a pot is like a bird in a cage," wrote Anon. That is all very well — for plants and for birds — if you have a garden, as Anon clearly did. But, in an age when so many of us live in apartments, to deny ourselves some plants in pots would be self-punishment indeed. And if you garden in a cold climate, the winter might seem even longer without cheerful pots in sunny windows. Some easy and colorful plants for centrally-heated houses and apartments include: Flowering Maple (*Abutilon hybridum*), slipper-wort (*Calceolaria*), nasturtium (*Tropaeolum*), Blue African Lily (*Agapanthus africanus*) and rosemary (*Rosmarinus*). All of these can be grown from seed.

16

17

18

19

20

21

22

23

Pocketbook flower (*Calceolaria herbeohybrida*).

If you haven't yet written off for seed and plant catalogs, do it now. Armchair gardening is a poor substitute for the real thing, but it has enormous attractions. All the seeds you sow one year germinate and make healthy plants the next. All the plants come up where you plant them, and *only* where you plant them. They come untouched through the late frosts of spring, and survive the predations of deer, rabbits or other local lovable beasts. They grow to the right height, flower at the right time, and make perfect color combinations with their neighbors. No staking is necessary. They do not suffer from mildew, black spot, earwigs, aphids, slugs or cutworm, so you can dispense with spraying and dusting and saucers of beer. They need no feeding, watering, mulching, dividing, deadheading or cutting down. You may be able to imagine this without any help, but plants grow better, outside of your imagination, in catalogs than anywhere else, and Paradise can be purchased for a few dollars or no charge at all.

24

25

26

27

28

29

PATRICIA THORPE

The cultivated "wild garden."

30

31

The modernist precept that form
follows function can usefully be
applied to plans for our garden.
What needs do we require our
gardens to serve? Are they for
entertaining, for children's play, for
relaxation, for the growing of
plants? These objectives are fortu-
nately not necessarily incompatible,
but it is important to think about
them as early in the planning process
as possible. We would not dream of
planning a public garden without
asking these questions; why should
we be less rigorous in thinking
about our own gardens?

Snowdrops

Daffodils may ''come before the swallow dares,'' but snowdrops come even earlier. If you live in a temperate climate, they come later as well! ''I should be greatly disappointed if this twentieth century,'' wrote E.A. Bowles in 1914, ''could not show me a Snowdrop at all times from late October until the advent of April brings so many other flowers that one scarcely notices their disappearance.'' It is unusual in North America to see any snowdrops other than the common snowdrop (*Galanthus nivalis*), its double form (*G.n. plenus*) and the larger Elwes' snowdrop (*G. elwesii*). In the north, they rarely flower before mid-February, and more typically in March and April, often pushing through the snow and earning their French name *perce-neige*, while farther south they may flower in January or earlier. Where they flower at the beginning of February, they are sometimes known as ''Candlemas bells'': ''The snowdrop in purest white arraie/First rears her head on Candlemas Day,'' and folklore tells that a weary Eve, fleeing with Adam from the Garden of Eden into a cold northern winter, was comforted by an angel who turned a snowflake into a snowdrop as a sign of returning spring and hope.

Both *G. nivalis* and *G. elwesii* are ideal for naturalizing, the first being particularly happy in damp, shady places, the second in drier, sunnier spots. For most people, a snowdrop is a snowdrop; but Elwes' snowdrop repays careful scrutiny, since the green markings on the inner petals (or *tepals* as the botanists now call them) vary considerably and are beautiful to contemplate. You can easily hasten the process of naturalization by digging the clumps ''in the green'' as they are finishing flowering and replanting immediately. Planted in a woodland setting where they do not have to compete with long grass, they will also self-sow. They are delightful as cut flowers, sweetly scented, and you do not have to peer around them to see your guests across the dinner table.

Snowdrops emerge through a crust of snow.

February

In gardening, as in other pastimes, there are frequently precise rules that make good sense to follow, but that are inconvenient because of other demands upon our time. So, here is some good news: there is no best time for sowing the seeds of perennial plants; everything depends upon your schedule and upon the facilities you have for looking after small seedlings. One important reason for sowing in the spring is that that is the time when seeds often become available, and if seeds have limited viability, then they had better be sown right away. A good example is the Pasqueflower (*Pulsatilla*), where germination is dependable only if the seed is sown as soon as it is ripe. But most seeds will stay viable for at least a year, which means that the Pasqueflower can be sown whenever we wish.

1

2

3

4

5

6

7

Lady of the Snow (*Pulsatilla vernalis*).

8

9

10

11

Glory-of-the-Snow (*Chionodoxa luciliae*).

12

13

14

15

Most books tell us to put our Christmas cacti (*Schlumbergera bridgesii*) outside in early fall, bringing them in before frost and then feeding the plants every two weeks or so. If your plants are not flowering well, you could try a variation that has produced good results: put the plants outside in a shady position as soon as the night temperature rarely falls below 10°C, and feed the plants every three weeks with a 30-10-10 fertilizer. When the plants come in, they need bright light (a north window in a sunny room is ideal), but the recommended temperatures of 20°C + during the day and 15°C + at night are unnecessarily high.

Winter aconites, Glory-of-the-Snow, Siberian squill, Spring Snowflake, the Naples onion, the Greek anemone, Spring Meadow Saffron, dog's tooth violet, Pretty Face, grape hyacinth, Arabian Star-of-Bethlehem, Lebanon squill — how is it possible to resist such names? As Elizabeth Lawrence wrote in *The Little Bulbs*, ''no garden is too small to hold them all if only a few of each are used, and no forest is too large to show them off if enough of one kind is planted.''

The winter aconites (*Eranthis hyemalis*), yellow cups on red stems above a green ruff, challenge the snowdrops, crocus and bulbous iris for the earliest place in the spring garden. They are not easy to establish, but try planting them among short grass or under shrubs or perennials, where they get some summer moisture. Will you laugh if I tell you that, in my early gardening days, I weeded out the Glory-of-the-Snow (*Chionodoxa luciliae*) seedlings since they looked so grass-like? Once you stop weeding them out, they multiply generously to fill a shrub bed with a sweep of small white-centered blue flowers.

16

17

18

19

20 *Prune Japanese Maple*
★ Treat Birch Trees!

21

22

23

Winter aconites (*Eranthis hyemalis*).

It is a well-known adage that more indoor plants are killed by over-watering than by watering insufficiently. Plants need both air and water at their roots. If the soil is continuously soaked, the air is squeezed out, the roots rot and the plant dies.

There is no infallible way to gauge the right amount of water. But most plants should be allowed to come close to drying out before they are watered. Better that a plant show occasional signs of distress from lack of water than that it sit in a marsh.

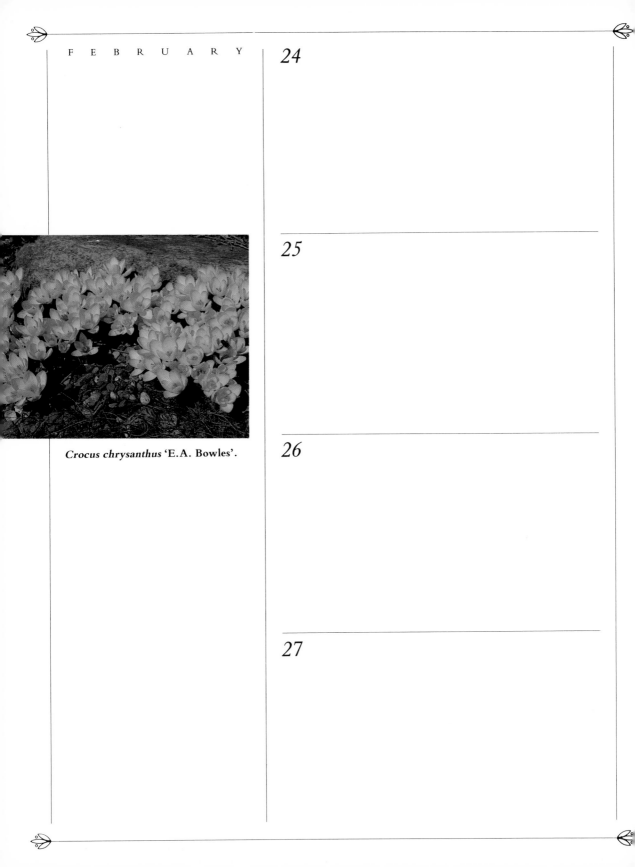

Crocus chrysanthus 'E.A. Bowles'.

24

25

26

27

29

Lady Byng at Government House

"Her Excellency's recipe for the making of a rock garden was sufficiently simple that it might be imitated by most garden lovers. She gathered her stones from the closest neighbourhood, which happened to be Rockcliffe Park. She planted all kinds of flowering plants from all corners of the globe, many of which she had collected for her gardens in England and in Canada. Then she added a plentiful selection of Canadian plants. In every individual case she had studied the native soil and surroundings of her plants, and then she sought to reproduce the home as closely as possible."

ALICE MACKAY,
CANADIAN HOMES AND GARDENS,
1926

Van Dusen Botanical Garden

The Van Dusen Garden, situated on 22 hectares of sandy, gravelly soil in southwest Vancouver, was created on the site of an abandoned golf course acquired in 1971; the garden was opened in 1975. The climate is, by the standards of most of Canada, mild, with an average July temperature of 17.4°C and an average January temperature of 2.4°C, though temperatures can dip considerably lower, and much damage can be done by sustained periods of subfreezing temperatures.

What has been accomplished since 1971 is remarkable. Though the garden is arranged systematically, with plants grouped by family or genus, or according to geographical origin, as befits a botanical garden, there is no sense that the beauty of the site and of the plantings has been sacrificed to research and pedagogical necessities, nor to the effort to develop as comprehensive a collection as possible of ornamental plants hardy in the area. The sense of garden has been underlined by the relative formality of the structure and plantings close to "the house," and the reduced formality as you move away from the entrance. There is, in fact, a formal garden, with granite walls, hedges of English boxwood and Hicks's yew, and rosebeds. But, as though to make sure that formality not become pomposity, there is, almost immediately adjacent, a children's garden with whimsical topiary and trees of "bizarre and unusual form," these latter recalling E.A. Bowles's "Lunatic Asylum": "the space which forms my home for demented plants."

Close by are gardens devoted to herbs, to plants of particular fragrance, to rock-garden plants "that can be grown without much difficulty in home gardens," and, of special interest to gardeners from east of the Rockies, to western North America flora. Here there is an enviable collection of dwarf and small conifers, including the elegant Brewer Spruce; mixed plantings of conifers and deciduous trees, along with native shrubs; and a stream bordered with species Iris, *Camassia*, and *Erythronium*.

If you wander northward, there are interesting collections of hollies, a somewhat unexpected Mediterranean Garden, plantings of viburnums and magnolias, and a garden of plants from the Southern Hemisphere. But this is Vancouver, and we have come to see the rhododendrons, so we walk west through the Heather Garden, and then south past the perennials and ornamental grasses and the summer-flowering hydrangeas, on to the Rhododendron Walk. Here many of the showy hybrids of the azalea section have been organized so as to show the way in which the hybrids have been developed over the last century.

We have time to note the obligatory (but no less enchanting) blue poppies in the Sino-Himalayan Garden, and to get lost for a few minutes in the Maze, before we begin the leisurely stroll around the north side of the ponds, with their collection of hardy water lilies, sedges and rushes, and where we can see the giant leaves of *Gunnera*, and so back to the entrance.

Van Dusen Botanical Garden
5251 Oak Street
Vancouver, B.C.
V6M 4H1
(604) 266-7194
Open seven days a week. Summer, 10:00 a.m. to 8:00 p.m.; winter, 10:00 a.m. to 4:00 p.m.

The Maze at Van Dusen Botanical Garden.

March

A Ramonda in the rock garden.

BARRIE PORTEOUS

1

2

3

4

5

Test whether the drainage in your garden is adequate by digging a hole 45 cm to 60 cm deep and filling it with water. If the water is still there a day later, remedial measures are called for. These may involve the installation of a proper (and expensive) drainage system, but a first step may be to try to improve the porosity of the soil by adding nondecomposable materials such as sand and gravel, while digging in compost, peat moss and bulky manure to improve its texture.

6

7

8

Many bulbs, including daffodils and tulips, form small bulbs, called "offsets," alongside the principal bulb. As the bulbs become crowded, flowers get smaller, and perhaps stop altogether. When this happens, the bulbs should be lifted in a clump with a fork, and the clump teased apart. All of the bulbs can then be replanted individually, but only the large ones will flower the following season. The smaller ones will throw up foliage until the bulbs have increased to flowering size; so, you must grow on the small bulbs for a year or two in a nursery bed or plant them where flowerless foliage for a year or two will not matter.

9

10

11

Saffron Crocus (*Crocus sativus*).

12

13

14

15

Starting seeds.

The serenity of a Japanese garden.

Spring

16

Spring Meadow Saffron
(*Bulbocodium vernum*).

17

18

19

Wild Blue Iris (*Iris versicolor*).

20

21
SPRING EQUINOX

22

23

The colors of spring are so predominantly yellow (aconites, *Iris danfordiae*, *Adonis*, *Narcissus*), blue (dwarf Iris, *Scilla*, *Chionodoxa*, *Puschkinia*) and white (snowdrops, *Scilla*, *Puschkinia*, daffodils) that it is a pleasure to have some other color. Five delightful exceptions to this triple rule are all pink, or nearly so. They include two tulips, *Tulipa pulchella*, which is not really pink but a rosy fuchsia, and *T. aucheriana*, which is a soft pink "like an old and rich brocade," wrote Vita Sackville-West. *Chionodoxa siehei* 'Pink Giant' is a real beauty, each stem producing many flowers of pale pink, unlike the more usual *Chionodoxa* blue.

A dog's-tooth violet (*Erythronium hendersonii*) from Oregon and California, but ruggedly hardy, has pink flowers with a lilac tint, a vivid maroon blotch at the throat and similarly colored anthers. The Spring Meadow Saffron (*Bulbocodium vernum*) has rosy-pink flowers with a white throat, the flowers produced low to the ground and hugged by dull green leaves. The bulbs should be dug and divided every three or four years.

24

Here are some attractive shrubs for
acid soils: azaleas and rhododendrons, heaths and heathers, camel-
lias, *Kerria*, *Hibiscus*, *Hydrangea*,
Tamarix, *Pieris* and magnolias. Some
heaths (varieties of *Erica carnea*) and
Magnolia stellata thrive nevertheless
on our alkaline soil.

25

26

27

28

29

30

31

Ankara crocus (*Crocus ancyrensis*).

Daffodils

Daffodils seem to be able to represent not only the arrival of spring (''that come before the swallow dares and take the winds of March with beauty'') but also its disappearance (''Fair daffodils, we weep to see you haste away so soon''). They have become so symbol-laden that it is tempting to mock: ''For oft when in my bath I lie/In vacant or in pensive nude . . . '' But we would not be without them, for they are almost trouble-free and provide generous bloom, both in the garden and as cut flowers for the house.

They are used in borders, where their flowers provide color before the perennials or annuals get under way, or are naturalized in grass. In borders, they are best planted in clumps of a dozen or more of one variety, and where their foliage will be obscured by neighboring plants. They seem to enjoy border conditions — a good amount of sun, protection by foliage from the worst heat of the summer, the watering and feeding destined for the perennials but from which they clearly benefit. I planted four dozen 'Beersheba' in a white bed (a totally unoriginal phase, but one that many gardeners need to pass through) in 1970, and this spring I picked off 220 flower heads. The best kind of fertilizer is one high in potash and phosphate, but low in nitrogen; bone meal is excellent. I sprinkle wood ash over all of our bulb plantings, but am never quite sure, when the bulbs do well, if it is because of the ash or in spite of it.

There are different theories about the best way to naturalize daffodils in grass. They can be planted in fairly tight clumps. For a more random effect, lob the bulbs gently toward a central marker, aiming to have the bulbs more densely clustered at the center, more sparsely scattered at the periphery, and plant them where they fall. 'February Gold', 'Mount Hood', *N. triandrus* 'Thalia' and the Pheasant's Eye narcissus have all done well. Try your favorites, but remember that doubles look clumsy at

**Daffodils and Snow Trillium
(*Trillium grandiflorum*).**

the best of times, and perhaps particularly so when naturalized. Ideally you should not cut the foliage for six weeks after flowering to allow the leaves to feed the bulb, so the grass cannot be cut during that time.

Yellow daffodils look lovely with white *Trillium grandiflorum* (give them both plenty of sun; you will be happily surprised at the results), whereas white daffodils associate well with the early purple foliage and pink-blue flowers of Virginia Bluebells (*Mertensia virginica*). The tiny species, such as *Narcissus bulbocodium*, *N. asturiensis*, *N. cyclamineus* and *N. triandrus*, have Spain and Portugal as their homelands, and are not reliably hardy in Zone 3. Where they are hardy, they naturalize well in thin damp grass and form exquisite dainty clumps in the rock garden. *Narcissus* 'Hawera,' a beautiful hybrid between *N. triandrus* and *N. jonquilla*, is hardy, grows to 20 to 22 cm and flowers when you think that you will have to wait another year to see a daffodil in bloom.

April

Cupflower (*Nierembergia repens*)
with Silver Thyme (*Thymus* ×
citriodorus 'Silver Queen').

1

2

3

5

6

7

Our interest in birds predates and has, to some extent, been displaced by our interest in gardening. Our first trees and shrubs were planted to attract birds; then we became fascinated by the shrubs. . . . We planted several kinds of mountain ash (*Sorbus*), honeysuckle shrubs (*Lonicera*), hawthorns (*Crataegus*), Snowberry (*Symphoricarpos albus*), Spindle tree (*Euonymus europaeus*), Wayfaring tree (*Viburnum lantana*), crab apples (*Malus*), Black Poplars (*Populus nigra*), American elder (*Sambucus canadensis*), Sea Buckthorn (*Hippophäe rhamnoides*), junipers (*Juniperus*) and Russian olive (*Elaeagnus angustifolius*); silverberry (*E. commutata*) would also have been attractive.

8

From The Grave Tree

Let me have a scarlet maple
For the grave-tree at my head,
With the quiet sun behind it,
In the years when I am dead.

       * * *

Scarlet when the April vanguard
Bugles up the laggard Spring
Scarlet when the bannered
   Autumn
Marches by unwavering.

       * * *

It will be my leafy cabin,
Large enough when June returns
And I hear the golden thrushes
Flute and hesitate by turns.

And in fall, some yellow
   morning,
When the stealthy frost has
   come,
Leaf by leaf it will befriend me
As with comrades going home.

BLISS CARMAN (1861–1929)

9

10

11

Common Blue Violet (*Viola papilionacea*).

12

13

14

15

Tulipa 'Maureen' and Evergreen Candytuft (*Iberis sempervirens*).

16

PAMELA HARPER

Fox-tail lilies (*Eremurus elwesii*).

17

18

When your *Eremurus* pushes its first fat fists through the earth, and if there is a possibility of frost to come, put an upturned bucket over it, or you may have to wait another year to enjoy its great flower spikes.

19

20

21

22

23

Most of us who live in northern climes are beginning to discover that dividing our plants in the fall is a risky business, that plants do not have time to re-establish themselves before winter descends and that losses are high. So, if your soil has begun to warm up, now is probably a good time to get started on the necessary business of division. Perennial plants, like wildflower meadows, are very much in vogue, especially among those who have little idea of how difficult they can be to cultivate successfully. Recently, I was asked to design a garden for a man who "had heard that there were plants that reappeared every year," and who wondered, like the good businessman that he is, whether they might be less expensive than annuals that need planting out every spring. After I had explained about soil preparation, feeding, deadheading, division, the occasional spraying, and the fact that most perennials have a vigorous flowering period of less than a month, he decided to stick with his annuals. For people who do not have much time to give to their garden, and who do not have help, that is not a bad idea. What is depressing is that these annuals invariably turn out to be geraniums, impatiens, begonias, marigolds and petunias.

24

25

26

27

PATRICIA THORPE

An inviting spot to sit and enjoy perennials in a northern garden.

29

30

Formal hedges must be clipped regularly to keep them dense and in shape. If they are not attended to, they quickly lose their grandeur. When the head gardener at Sissinghurst, in England, went off to the Second World War, he said to his employer: "Look after the hedges. We can get the rest back later." Good formal hedges can be made from the English holly (*Ilex aquifolium*, Z6); Amur privet (*Ligustrum amurense* Z3), or its handsome but more tender relative, California privet (*L. ovalifolium*), especially in its variety 'Aureum'; European hornbeam (*Carpinus betulus*, Z5) or its American sibling (*C. caroliniana*, Z2), neither of which is an evergreen, but both of which retain their fall leaves well into the winter; white cedar or American arborvitae (*Thuja occidentalis*, Z2), which may lose some of its greenness during the winter, but with proper care will make a thick hedge from the ground up; and best of all, the yews (English yew, *Taxus baccata*, Z6; Japanese yew, *T. cuspidata*, Z3; and the cross between them, *T.* × *media*, Z4) that make us think of rain-drenched English and northern Italian gardens, but actually tolerate a wide variety of growing conditions.

Tulips

During the course of a year, my memory of a particular plant at flowering time fades like a photograph left in the sun. This is sad, like the diminution of friendship, but offers the pleasure of renewed acquaintance. In the winter, I may say to myself, ''How beautiful the tulips were last spring,'' but I am remembering less their beauty than that I found them beautiful. I was reminded of this separation between the instantaneous perception of beauty and its recollection in tranquility when the first flower of *Tulipa linifolia* unfolded in this morning's crisp April sunshine. I thought I had seen a brown thrasher a little earlier, and now I could hear it. Its repeated attempts to get started on, first this aria, and then that, reminded me of my own shower recitals when I may start off as Boris Christoff singing Philip II in *Don Carlos*, broaden my scope to Merrill and Bjoerling doing the famous Pearl Fishers' duet, and then, as humidity works its tricks, bring in all four solo voices in the Verdi *Requiem*. As I went to get a good look at my fellow vocalist, my attention was diverted by a brilliant patch of color.

Tulipa linifolia has a small flower, as tulips go, about 5 cm across, not quite flat, the petals scalloped to a point, like the entrance to a Turkish courtyard. The color is a shiny, blazing red, but what makes the flower entrancing is the contrast of this red with a small purple blotch at the center, and with the purple anthers, which, as the flower opens, lie along the petals and point toward their tips.

I have a passion for the species tulips, and try to add one or two kinds each year. *Tulipa pulchella* comes early in a range of rosy colors, and has an outstanding white form with a central blotch of darkest red and a powerful fragrance. It is soon followed by the yellow flowers with bronze exteriors of *T. urumiensis* and its white-tipped companion, *T. tarda*. *T. schrenkii* is aggressively handsome in red, gold and black. There is a wide

choice. The plants are mostly under 30 cm at flowering time, though all leave behind tall and unsightly foliage. Plant the species tulips in early fall as soon as they are available. They are best in clumps, 5 to 7 cm apart, and 12 to 15 cm deep. Given a spot where they receive good moisture in spring and then a summer's baking, and where they can be protected from rodents, they will gladden your heart for many years.

Tulipa linifolia and *Alyssum montanum.*

May

Beautybush (*Kolkwitzia amabilis*).

1

2

3

4

5

6

7

From The St. Lawrence and the Saguenay

The Spring is gone — light,
genial-hearted Spring!
Whose breath gives odor to the
violet,
Crimsons the wild rose, tints the
blackbird's wing,
Unfolds the buttercup. Spring
that has set
To music the laughter of the
rivulet,
Sent warm pulsations through the
hearts of hills,
Reclothed the forests, made the
valleys wet
With pearly dew, and waked the
grave old mills
From their calm sleep, by the
loud rippling of the rills.

CHARLES SANGSTER
(1822–1893)

Wild lily of the valley (*Maianthemum canadense*).

"I soon found beauties in my forest wanderings in the unknown trees and plants of the forest. These things became a great resource, and every flower and shrub and forest tree awakened an interest in my mind. . . . They became like dear friends, soothing and cheering, by their unconscious influence, hours of loneliness and hours of sorrow and suffering. . . . The only book I had access to was an old edition of a "North American Flora" by Frederick Pursh. . . . My next teachers were old settlers' wives, and choppers and Indians. These gave me knowledge of another kind. . . . Having no resource in botanical works on our native Flora, save what I could glean from Pursh, I relied entirely upon my own powers of observation, and this did very much to enhance my interest in my adopted country and add to my pleasure, as a relief . . . from the home longings that arise in the heart of the exile."

MRS. C.P. TRAILL,
STUDIES OF PLANT LIFE IN CANADA, OR GLEANINGS FROM FOREST, LAKE AND PLAIN,
1885

8

9

10

11

12

13

14

15

Well-maintained lawns — perhaps substitutes for the pond or lake we do not have?

Dwarf Goldenrod (*Solidago nemoralis*).

16

Tulipa aucheriana.

Here is an elegant first course for a spring lunch.

Asparagus With Asparagus Mayonnaise

1.25 kg fresh asparagus
250 mL cup mayonnaise

Trim and peel asparagus and boil in salted water. Do not overcook. Drain. Cool the asparagus and arrange 1 kg on a serving dish. Puree the remaining 0.25 kg asparagus, and mix well into the mayonnaise. Serve the asparagus and pass the mayonnaise in a sauceboat. Serves 4.

17

18

19

20

21

22

23

A friend asked me why the shrubs in her garden never flowered. The shrubs were lilacs and mock oranges. Every fall, a gardening service came to the garden and pruned the shrubs heavily in order "to encourage strong bushy growth in the spring." What the service also did was to prune away the flowering stems. This reminds us that shrubs such as lilacs, mock oranges, forsythia and flowering currant should be pruned after flowering, when the shoots on which the flowers have appeared can be cut back to fresh growth on the main branches. It also reminds us that not all gardening services are reliable.

Shrubs that flower later in the summer, such as Potentilla, *Caryopteris*, *Tamarix*, smoke tree, *Clethra* and rose of Sharon, should be pruned firmly in early spring.

Wild Columbine
(*Aquilegia canadensis*).

Much of Canada should be closed
from January through March. There
would be signs at the U.S. border:
"Fermeture annuelle — closed until
spring," and we would all go for
three months to Florida or California or New Zealand or Monaco. Or,
of course, to British Columbia —
that part, at least, that lies along the
Pacific. While most of Canada is
covered in snow, Vancouver has a
January *average* temperature above
freezing, and to a visitor from
Portage and Main, Victoria feels
subtropical. If you are looking for a
tan, you would be better on the ski-
slopes (and one of the great
injustices is that, in Vancouver, you
are only a short drive from some of
Canada's best skiing conditions), but
if the holiday from the garden,
enforced by your soil being frozen
to a depth of half-a-metre or more,
is depressing you, then Go West,
young would-be gardener. Take a
trowel — and an umbrella.

24

25

26

27

28

29

30

31

A Mexican phlox (*Phlox* 'Mary Maslin').

While many gardeners lament their sunless gardens, a garden without shade would lose in brilliance for want of contrast. Though deep shade — that of a beech forest, for example — makes growing anything very difficult, filtered shade or even a high canopy of leaves that permits much light has many possibilities. Some good perennials for shady places are: *Acanthus*, monkshood (*Aconitum*), Baneberry (*Actaea*), Lady's Mantle (*Alchemilla*), *Anemone*, columbines (*Aquilegia*), *Bergenia*, many campanulas, Snakeroot (*Cimicifuga*), lily of the valley (*Convallaria*), *Corydalis*, and we are only at "C" . . .

Annuals

Now is the time to sally forth to your local garden center and stock up on annual plants. Annuals have great advantages over perennials because they give immediate color (many annuals can be purchased in flower), require less care, and in many cases flower from the time you buy them until the first frost. They can be used to fill gaps in your perennial borders, be grown in pots that can be moved around the garden to strategic points or brought into the house for indoor color or be planted in hanging baskets. They can be planted in ordinary soil, may need to be shaded for a day or two if the weather is hot, will ask to be watered from time to time, will benefit from individual dead-heading and a collective shearing if they become unattractively leggy and can be thrown on to the compost heap at the end of the season.

With such a catalog of virtues, who could complain? Each year the nursery industry tells us that more and more varieties are becoming available. Sadly, these appear to be mostly new varieties of the same old standbys. So, we have pink impatiens with golden variegation on the foliage, marigolds whose yellow makes mustard look discreet, petunias in lovely colors but which collapse in soggy mounds at the first good downpour, zinnia with all the charm of an infantry unit on parade, alyssum and *Nierembergia* to edge our and everyone else's beds. I love the white cleomes and white cosmos that are sometimes available, but do we need one more salmon *Pelargonium* (geranium)? We can't blame the nursery trade for this; they give us what we want. And we buy these varieties because they are there, which saves us the trouble of starting our own.

But if we have the time and a good seed catalogue, and are prepared to take a little trouble, there is a wealth of possibilities. Most annuals are easy to germinate, either sown directly in the garden or started in flats for transplanting. Here are a few that

Blue Pimpernel (*Anagallis linifolia*).

we have grown or seen grown with great success: California Poppies, Scarlet Flax, the dwarf Meadow Foam (*Limnanthes douglasii*), the Mask Flower (*Alonsoa warscewiczii*), Tidy Tips (*Layia elegans*), and the ravishing Blue Pimpernel (*Anagallis linifolia*), which may be perennial in warm regions, but an annual which reseeds itself for most of us. All of these need sunny positions. For shady places, try Baby-Blue-Eyes (was there ever a better reason for using a botanical name, *Nemophila menziesii*?), *Viola* 'Bowles' Black', the lime-green *Nicotiana langsdorfii*, the biennial white Honesty (*Lunaria annua*), and the Monkey flower (*Mimulus variegatus*) for moist semishade.

We are constantly being counseled to avoid spottiness in our gardens by planting in large drifts. This may be sensible if we are planting annuals, which will continue to be attractive for a long period throughout the summer and into the fall. Even then, if we have a small garden, a large drift or two may take up most of the space, so that we are not able to indulge any taste for variety. The problem is worsened if we follow the current vogue for perennials, most of which flower for only a few weeks. If we plant them in masses, what shall we do when they are no longer in flower? The answer may lie in finding plants with good foliage and with "architectural" and structural features. Here are some suggestions: hostas, which come in all sizes and with great variation in leaf coloration; the great biennial Scotch thistle (*Onopordon acanthium*), which grows easily to 180 to 200 cm, is almost as wide and has gray foliage; the mulleins, with their rough, pointed leaves and tall spikes of white or yellow flowers; *Crambe maritima*, the kale of our table, with low-growing wide-spreading silvery leaves, and its large cousin, *C. cordifolia*, with its masses of white baby's-breath–like flowers on 150 cm stems in June and July; and *Sedum* 'Autumn Joy,' which is attractive in foliage and flower for much of the year.

June

1

2

3

4

5

6

7

Crambe cordifolia.

Daylily (*Hemerocallis fulva*).

8

9

10

11

**White Oriental poppies with blue
and white perennial geraniums.**

12

13

14

15

What would we do without the perennial geraniums? In most cases easily hardy to Zone 3, they come in flowers of blue and pink, lavender and white, magenta and rose. The plants generally form mounds of finely dissected foliage that tend to sprawl in the larger varieties and forms. They have a long flowering period throughout June and much of July and, when flowering is over, will form compact mounds once again if cut back rather severely. The mounds can be 60 to 75 cm high. There are also delightful candidates for the rock garden of not more than a few centimetres in height and spread. They all seem to thrive best in something less than full sun, and in a not-too-dry spot.

Moth Mullein (*Verbascum blatteria*).

Clematis 'Sir Garnet Wolseley' and
Beautybush (*Kolkwitzia amabilis*).

Summer

From June

Gone are the wind-flower and the
    adder-tongue,
And the sad drooping bellwort,
    and no more
The snowy trilliums crowd the
    forest floor;
The purpling grasses are no
    longer young,
And summer's wide-set door
O'er the thronged hills and the
    broad panting earth
Lets in the torrent of the later
    bloom,
Haytime, and harvest, and the
    after mirth,
The slow soft rain, the rushing
    thunder plume.

ARCHIBALD LAMPMAN
(1861–1899)

16

17

18

19

21
SUMMER SOLSTICE

Growing labels.

22

23

Peonies.

24

25

26

27

28

29

30

More perennials for shady places:
Lady's-slipper (*Cypripedium*), Bleed-
ing Heart (*Dicentra*); *Epimedium*;
some euphorbias, *Geranium* (the
hardy kinds, not to be confused
with our tender bedding-out plant,
Pelargonium); *Helleborus*; daylilies
(*Hemerocallis*); *Hosta*; *Kirengeshoma
palmata*; *Lobelia cardinalis*; Musk
Mallow (*Malva moschata*), which,
though it grows freely in sun along
our roadsides, will do well in some
shade and is worthy of an invitation
into the garden; and the glorious
and tricky species of *Meconopsis*.

Yellow Lady's-slipper (*Cypripedium calceolus*).

Montreal Botanical Garden

The Montreal Botanical Garden, one of the world's great botanical gardens, was founded in 1931 by Brother Marie-Victorin, appropriately one of Canada's greatest botanists. The 73 hectares contain about 26 000 species and varieties, organized into a series of specialized gardens designed to exemplify the garden's primary objectives: horticulture, particularly as it relates to the Montreal region, but also focusing on unusual plants; botany, reflecting the garden's commitment to research and teaching, by emphasizing the diversity of the plant world and by calling attention to rare and endangered species; ethnobotany, or plants that have a special nonornamental relation to man; and design and landscaping.

An impressive entrance driveway, bordered by large beds devoted to spring bulbs and then annuals, leads past a fountain and water staircase to the administrative building. Behind it lie the great conservatories, some used for research, which house the magnificent collections of orchids, begonias, gesneriads, and bonsai and penjing. The central conservatory is given over to spectacular seasonal flower exhibits, each devoted to a special theme: "Spring in Greece," "English Countryside," and so on.

The outdoor areas include fine perennial beds, concentrating on plants suitable for the Montreal region and Eastern Canada. We pass through them to a collection of economic plants, plants that are of particular usefulness to man, and on to the test gardens for vegetables and annuals. The Physic Garden is next. It has been subdivided into a Monastery Garden, where we find herbs that were grown by the monks of the Middle Ages; a Medicinal Plant Garden, embracing both the plants of folklore and those valued by the pharmaceutical industry; and a Poisonous Plant Garden, where you can plot your enemies' destruction.

There are displays of hedges and ground covers, shade and

MONTRÉAL BOTANICAL GARDEN

bog gardens, dwarf conifers (and some large ones; the Dawn
Redwood, *Metasequioa glyptostroboides*, must surely here be at
the northern limits of its range?), heaths and rhododendrons,
many of the plants surprising us with their hardiness. The garden
is also famous for its educational work with children, a section
of the grounds being given over to plots where children can
make their first supervised efforts at gardening.

Montreal Botanical Garden
4101, rue Sherbrooke est
Montréal, PQ
H1X 2B2
(514) 872-1400
Outdoor gardens open seven days a week, from 8:00 a.m. to dusk.
Conservatories open seven days a week, from 9:00 a.m. to 6:00 p.m.

July

On a visit to England some years ago, I bought a lily from a nursery as a present for a friend. The lily was the double form of the well-known Tiger Lily (*Lilium tigrinum*), producing glowing orange-red flowers with six petals instead of the three found on the single form, and flowering late into August, which makes it a very useful contributor to late-summer color. Later that year, my friend sent me some of the bulbils, the small bulbs that form in the leaf axils (where the side shoots join the main stem). I planted them in ordinary soil in small boxes, and left them to grow on during the winter, and then planted them out in a nursery bed in the spring. Two years later, they were flowering in our garden. This process can be speeded up by removing the flower buds from the parent plant; then the bulbils will grow larger as they ripen. This lily is said to prefer a lime-free soil, but it grows happily in our garden on a limestone escarpment.

1

CANADA DAY

2

3

4

5

6

7

Kansas Gayfeather (*Liatris pychnostachya*) in front of the White Rose-Campion (*Lychnis coronaria alba*).

Plants grow between stone steps.

8

9

10

11

12

13

14

15

Wind is the great enemy of fragrance in the garden, so if you are trying to make a scented garden you must look for a sheltered spot. One of the great advantages of making "rooms" within a garden is that the walls or hedges that delineate those rooms provide calm spaces to be filled by fragrance. The list of fragrant flowers and shrubs is without end: roses, of course, especially the "old-fashioned" kinds, though some modern cultivars are also very fragrant; many of the climbing honeysuckles; lavenders; lilies, particularly the Oriental hybrids, which have the secondary advantage of flowering later than most other lilies; lily of the valley; cyclamen; *Acidanthera bicolor*; annual Sweet Alyssum (*Lobularia maritima*); almost all the pinks (*Dianthus*); *Gardenia*, jasmine, and the clove currant (*Ribes odoratum*); *Magnolia*, Mexican orange (*Choisya ternata*, Z7), and every *Daphne* I have met; the Pheasant's Eye daffodil (*Narcissus poeticus*); and three of the best-loved annuals, sweet pea (*Lathyrus odoratus*), mignonette (*Reseda odorata*) and night-scented stock (*Matthiola bicornis*).

Purple Honeysuckle
(*Lonicera hispidula*).

I always pot up some Regal lilies, so that I can set them at the back door just as they start to open their flowers, which is about now, and where they capture everyone's attention, not just with their long yellow-throated white trumpets, but with their heady fragrance. Not everyone enjoys the same scents; the sweeter-than-hawthorn–like fragrance from the flowers of the Japanese lilac arouses mixed reactions. Anyone who loves the fragrance of nicotine (*Nicotiana alata*) — and that means almost everyone — and who has plenty of space, should try one of its relatives, *N. sylvestris*. This is an imposing plant with large basal foliage, and 150 cm stems clad in hanging white flowers that save their fragrance for twilight. It grows best in slightly moist shade. It is an annual, alas, except for Argentinians and people who live in equivalent climates.

16

17

18

19

20

21

22

23

A Tobacco plant (*Nicotiana sylvestris*).

24

Clematis 'Gravetye Beauty' and
'Huldine' in July.

25

26

If Thou Wouldest Roses Scent

If thou wouldest *Roses Scent*
Mend, and make more excellent,
Then thou formerly hadst them,
Plant but Garlick to their Stem;
Likewise, if a Friend of thine
Should to Goodness so incline,
As to lead a Vertuous life,
Let him take a Scolding Wife:
Thus Natura works, you see
Sometimes by Antipathy

FRANCIS DANIEL PASTORIUS

(1651–1720)

27

28

29

30

31

One of the most useful items among my gardening aids is a plastic cone, 25 cm high, with an open bottom 18 cm in diameter and an open top 2.5 cm across. The plastic is clear, with vertical green stripes and with tabs at the bottom, which makes it possible to tether the cone firmly to the ground with a couple of twigs. Whenever I plant out small seedlings, or move larger plants, I cover them with a cone, both to reduce the intensity of the sun and to keep in moisture and retain humidity. The cone protects seedlings from wind and from most crawling insects. I also sometimes staple the top of the cone to keep rain from falling on woolly-leaved plants, which dislike moisture resting on their leaves. Try your local source of gardening supplies.

Canada Anemone (*Anemone canadensis*).

Clematis

There is a strange mystique about clematis (quite aside from how the word should be pronounced and what its plural form should be), suggesting that they are difficult to grow and require special conditions or special gardening skills. Some will not survive extreme cold, though some of the most beautiful are to be found in the harsher regions of Northern Europe and Canada, and perhaps great heat can be a problem, though we grow thirty large-flowered hybrids and species in a small enclosed part of the garden where the temperature in the sun must frequently exceed 38°C. But if you want ''secrets'' for success, there are three. You must first dig a hole 60 cm deep and 45 cm wide, and fill that hole with ''good stuff'' — a mixture of manure and compost and topsoil. The rule of adding lime is an Old Spouses' Tale, perpetuated by ignorant nurserypeople. Into this hole you will plant your clematis with great care and tenderness. You must give the plant something to climb on; a trellis of some kind is best for the hybrids, but most of the species love to scramble through a shrub. And finally, at least once a week, take a book, a chair and a hose out to the garden, place the hose, trickling slowly, at the base of the clematis, and sit and read for twenty minutes. With thirty clematis, that makes for a good ten hours' work.

The large-flowered hybrids — × *jackmanii*, 'Nelly Moser', 'Ramona', 'Niobe', and so on — are relatively easy to come by and provide exuberant displays, but much recent attention has been turning toward the species, of which there are about 250. These are frequently robust and exquisite: the yellow *tangutica* with seed heads as attractive as its long-petaled flowers; the purples and reds of the nodding, star-shaped *viticella*; the garden-filling perfumes of the vigorous *flammula* and *maximowicziana*, both producing masses of small white flowers, the first in early August, the second in early September.

Clematis macropetala in late spring.

August

Most of us race through our
necessary weeding as quickly as
possible, there being more important
things, inside the garden and out,
that require our attention. But if
you can take the time to weed
slowly and with care, there are at
least two rewards.

The first is the very practical one,
that among the weeds may be
concealed some desirable seedlings
from your treasured plants. Just this
morning I found half a dozen small
plants of the bright yellow-flowered
gray-foliaged *Eriophyllum lanatum*, a
plant that seems not to have a
sensible common name but that you
will be happy to have in your dry
sunny garden for its long period of
generous bloom from late June
onward. They will be transplanted
or potted up as presents for friends.

But there are also the contempla-
tive pleasures of sitting or kneeling
quietly in the garden, seeing the
garden close up, feeling the soil
under your fingers, not rushing,
with a mind largely free for
reflection. I have sorted out quite a
few professional and personal concerns while easing the grass out
from around the asparagus.

1

2

3

4

5

6

7

***Phlox subulata* 'Red Wings'.**

If your garden has ugly surrounds that you wish to conceal as much as possible from the windows of the house, or the terrace or deck, remember that trees, fences and walls placed close to the viewer will succeed more completely at blocking out the view than those placed close to the offending objects.

8

9

10

11

Raised beds with clematis and alpines.

Raised beds are much in vogue, and with good reason. They are ideal for growing small plants (and so form a convenient substitute for a rock garden), which can then be seen and weeded around without back spasms, or for growing plants that require special conditions that you cannot otherwise supply, such as rapid drainage in a garden on clay or acidity in a garden that is predominantly alkaline. If the beds are constructed at the correct height and are not too wide, they can make gardening possible for someone confined to a wheelchair.

12

13

14

15

The Midsummer Garden

In time the tender peas
will ripen and be eaten,
the roses infinite
of bronze and silver beaten
their fiery dew release;
each flecked and flickered minute

will nest itself in alders
and hanging, whitely glitter,
the cats will seek the shade
too lazy to pursue,
the rhubarb will grow bitter,
the earth too dry to spade.

* * *

With leafmould and with burrs,
with broken stalks and spears,
I bury seed that stirs
deep in the garden's years,
and by this act I prove
myself the tool of love.

MIRIAM WADDINGTON,
COLLECTED POEMS,
1986

It is difficult to use flowering shrubs for formal hedges, since clipping will remove many of the flowering branches. Nothing looks more dismal than tightly clipped hedges of *Spiraea* or *Forsythia* with the occasional flower looking like a prisoner behind bars. But there are many shrubs, including the two just mentioned, which can be used to make delightful informal hedges. Winged Euonymus (*Euonymus alata*, Z3) provide a wonderful streak of scarlet in the fall garden, while various bush honeysuckles produce their rose and pink flowers in early summer. Among the barberries, Rosemary Barberry (*Berberis* × *stenophylla*, Z5) thrives in sun or light shade, its arching branches bearing golden flowers in spring and purple berries in the fall. We have been experimenting with the Red-leaf Rose (*Rosa glauca*), which has gray rather than red leaves, winsome soft-pink flowers, and splendid bright-red hips and plum foliage in the fall. Mock oranges have the advantage of fragrance, and come in all sizes from the 275 cm Sweet Mock orange (*Philadelphus coronarius*) to the charming and compact *Philadelphus* × 'Manteau d'Hermine'. Glossy Abelia (*Abelia* × *grandiflora*) has long been a favorite where the winters are not too hard (Z6).

16

17

18

19

20

21

22

23

A low-growing Evening Primrose (*Oenothera triloba*).

A third crop of perennials for shady places: Virginia Bluebell (*Mertensia virginica*); forget-me-nots (*Myosotis*); Chinese Lanterns (*Physalis franchetii*), but well away from your treasured plants; Solomon's-seal (*Polygonatum × hybridum*); *Primula*; Lungwort (*Pulmonaria*); *Tiarella*; *Trillium*; and the imposing but rarely seen *Veratrum*. Many types of *Viola* will seed themselves, sometimes a little too joyously.

24

25

26

27

Eriophyllum lanatum.

28

29

30

31

One of the best gifts you could give to a youngster who has a few square metres of soil ready for planting would be a zucchini plant or two. Hardly anything else in the garden grows as vigorously while being more or less continuously neglected. There are flowers; there are fruit; and the fruit can be turned over to the chef in the family to make a zucchini pie.

Zucchini Pie

2 zucchini, unpeeled (about 1 kg)
45 mL olive oil
1 onion, minced
125 mL grated Parmesan, plus
   45 mL
160 mL cup cooked rice
1 egg, beaten
parsley
salt and pepper

Preheat the oven to 190°C. Dice the zucchini. Heat the olive oil in a frying pan and cook the onion slowly, until tender. Add the zucchini and cook gently, stirring occasionally. Pour off some of the liquid, and allow to cool somewhat.

Stir the rice, 125 mL Parmesan, egg, parsley, salt and pepper into the pan, then turn the mixture into a shallow, oiled baking dish. Sprinkle with the remaining cheese and a little of the olive oil. Bake for 20 minutes. Serves 6.

Old Roses

We don't grow many roses, partly because roses are labor-intensive at the times when we are least able to attend to them, but also because the garden has sandy, gravelly, alkaline soil that water passes through almost instantaneously, and roses are not at their happiest in dry conditions. Peter Beales, an English rose expert writes that "roses tend to do rather better in slightly acid soils and have a definite preference for clay." We can offer neither, so we enjoy roses mostly in other people's gardens.

And what roses there are to enjoy! Since I grow roses only in my mind's eye, I shall not choose them for their color, but for their names and their associations, and hope that they are full with fragrance:

> Footfalls echo in the memory
> Down the passage which we did not take
> Towards the door we never opened
> Into the rose garden.

I shall have a corner devoted to the departed aristocrats, to 'Mary Queen of Scots', 'William III', 'Lady Curzon' and various 'Ducs de this-and-that'. Since I am in my snobbish mode, I shall pass on 'Daisy Hill', 'Sealing Wax', 'Eddie's Crimson' and 'Phoebe's Frilled Pink'. 'La Mortola' will make me think of a great Italian garden, and 'Highdownensis' of a great English one. To persuade you that I am not parochial, I shall include 'Frühlingszauber' (which I think means "Spring magic"), but not the ugly-sounding 'Frühlingsanfang' ("Spring's beginning").

'Dresden Doll' and 'Belle Amour' or 'The Tipsy Imperial Concubine' may explain the naming of 'Rambling Rector'. 'Meg Merrilees' sounds like fun, but I shall include her only if I can have some Musk roses ('Princess of Nassau' has flowers of "yellowish-straw, very sweet"), some Gallicas ('Red Rose of Lancaster' will do very nicely), but then I had better include

Rosa × *alba*, the 'White Rose of York'. Who could leave out 'Maiden's Blush', known also by its saucier French form as 'Cuisse de Nymphe' or 'Cuisse de Nymphe Émue' in its "more richly coloured clones"? Where shall I put 'Blanc Double de Coubert', or our native *Rosa nitida* with the ambivalent recommendation of "hips small, oval and slightly bristly"? 'Chapeau de Napoléon' is a Moss rose with "highly scented, cabbage-like, silvery deep pink flowers" with "a fascinating moss formation on the calyx" that looks like a cocked hat. My final choice is *R. maximowicziana* because there is a clematis with the same specific name which I have diligently learned to pronounce. Whatever your criterion for selection, you can see many of the older roses at Queen Elizabeth Park, in Vancouver; Assiniboine Park, in Winnipeg; the Royal Botanical Gardens, in Hamilton; Edwards Gardens, in Toronto; the Montreal Botanical Garden; and the Historic Gardens at Annapolis Royal.

French rose (*Rosa gallica*).

September

Red Pepper Jelly

375 mL sweet red pepper
125 mL green hot pepper
375 mL cider vinegar
150 g pectin
1250 mL sugar

Put washed, chopped peppers into
the blender with the vinegar and
blend thoroughly. Combine with
sugar in a large pan. Bring to a boil,
then allow to boil for 2 minutes.
Add pectin; skim. Pour into steril-
ized jars. Wonderful with cold meats.

1

2

3

Painted Trillium (*Trillium undulatum*).

4

5

6

7

**One of the many attractively
foliaged hostas.**

8

Black-eyed Susan (*Rudbeckia hirta*) along a streamside.

9

10

11

12

13

14

15

From **Tecumseh**

This region is as lavish of its
    flowers
As Heaven of its primrose blooms
    by night.

This is the Arum, which within
    its root
Folds life and death; and this the
    Prince's Pine,
Fadeless as love and truth — the
    fairest form
That ever sun-shower washed
    with sudden rain.
This golden cradle is the
    Moccasin Flower,
Wherein the Indian hunter sees
    his hound;
And this dark chalice is the
    Pitcher-Plant,
Stored with the water of
    forgetfulness;
Whoever drinks of it, whose heart
    is pure,
Will sleep for aye 'neath foodful
    asphodel,
And dream of endless love.

CHARLES MAIR
(1838–1927)

Evening Primrose
(*Oenothera biennis*).

Morning shadows.

Autumn

16

Troubled with aphids? If you don't like to spray, how about trying lacewing fly larvae. ''It feeds voraciously on aphids, piercing their bodies with its sharp mouth parts and sucking out their body fluids after first injecting digestive enzymes to liquefy the aphid's organs and a tranquillizer to minimize struggling'' (Nancy Wilkes Bubel, *The Adventurous Gardener*). Maybe you'd rather have aphids.

17

18

Red Baneberry (*Actaea rubra*).

19

20

21

AUTUMNAL EQUINOX

PAMELA HARPER

Rosa 'Blanc Double de Coubert'.

22

23

The hot colors of high summer.

Butterflies are one of the joys of the summer garden. Some plants that attract butterflies are: bayberry (*Myrica pensylvanica*), goldenrod (*Solidago*), Mountain-Laurel (*Kalmia latifolia*), Honesty (*Lunaria*), heliotrope (*Heliotropium*), cinquefoil (*Potentilla*), Michaelmas daisy (*Aster*), *Spiraea*, lavender (*Lavandula*), hawthorns (*Crataegus*), lilac (*Syringa*), pinks (*Dianthus*), thyme (*Thymus*), and, above all, the Butterfly Bush (*Buddleia davidii*).

24

25

26

27

28

29

30

Crocus, especially the small-flowered species, should be allowed to make rivulets of gold and blue and yellow through the rock garden, where they can be planted under chicken wire that has been tucked under the rocks and then covered with gravel to prevent chipmunks and squirrels from digging them up. *Ornithogalums* produce white flowers, sometimes with amusing black anthers, but be careful of *O. umbellatum*, known around here as "The Dreaded Umbellatum" because of its invasive propensities. Beware, too, the grape hyacinth, which will infiltrate your prize alpines, and the white Naples onion (*Allium neapolitanum*), which will inevitably turn out to be a different *Allium* and of a particularly dowdy pink. The dog's tooth violet *grows* in shade but *flowers* in sun; if you plant it in a very shady place, you will have lots of leaves but few flowers.

Siberian squill (*Scilla sibirica*) is an old-time favorite, in blue and white. Just around the corner, there is a steep bank at the foot of some gardens that must have been made eighty years ago. Someone planted *Scilla*, and in May the bank is a dense carpet of blue, brilliant enough to slow the traffic.

Vegetables

It used to be so difficult to obtain unusual vegetables that the only way to have them was to grow them oneself. In many areas that has changed, and the proliferation of good vegetable stores has brought vegetables to our doorsteps that we used earlier only to meet on our travels. But not everyone is fortunate in this way. Our desire to have access to the very freshest vegetables, the sense that we are doing something physically — and perhaps spiritually — healthy, and our concerns about the use of pesticides and chemical fertilizers in commercial vegetable production may encourage us to grow our own.

Most vegetables need good soil, sun and moisture, so that if you have a small garden they will compete for space with the ornamental plants. Lettuce can perhaps be grown in your perennial beds since it is an early crop and can be substantially consumed before the perennials really hit their stride, and strawberries have long been used as an edging plant. One way of reducing the competition is to make your vegetable garden ornamental, that is, to think about giving it form and definition, texture and color by defining the limits of the bed — perhaps dividing it into symmetric sections with low hedges? Some forms of lavender are certainly hardy to Zone 4, Lavender cotton (*Santolina chamaecyparissus*) and Germander (*Teucrium chamaedrys*) to Zone 5. Lavender could be left unclipped; the two latter respond well to clipping. If you have space, the sections could be further divided by small paths firm enough to support your wheelbarrow. Into these sections you can plant your *arugula*, *radicchio*, purple basil, sweet gourmet carrots, plum tomatoes tied to posts, blue-flowered salsify interplanted with your favorite fast-maturing lettuce, and Italian eggplant that will make an aubergine pie to melt the stoniest heart. And if you are a disciple of companion plantings, you can do away with those dreadful spindly rows of marigolds, and plant a whole section or two, boldly, and hope that works as well.

What I have in mind . . .
Villandry, France.

October

I learn from a book on Chinese plants, *The Alpine Plants of China*, that *Rheum palmatum*, an ornamental rhubarb, "is used as a medicine for curing pyretic toxin, breaking up various forms of congestion, dissolving extravasated blood, curing constipation caused by real internal heat, dysentery, dropsy, bloodshot eyes, headache, and amenorrhoea. Used externally, it can cure carbuncles, malignant boils and scalds and burns." I don't know what some of these ailments are, but this is clearly a useful plant to have around.

1

2

3

4

5

6

7

PAMELA HARPER

Sorrel Rhubarb (*Rheum palmatum*).

Gravel used as a setting for rock garden plants.

Eggplant Pie

1 kg eggplant
225 g sliced mozzarella cheese
Parmesan for topping
375 mL tomato sauce
olive oil
salt and pepper
flour

Peel the eggplant and cut into long thin slices. Salt them and place in colander to drain for 1 hour. Dry them, then dust with flour and fry gently in olive oil. Drain on paper towels. Put a little oil in the bottom of an ovenproof dish. Add a layer of eggplant, cover with thin slices of cheese, then tomato sauce, repeating until all the eggplant slices have been used. Top with grated Parmesan and a sprinkling of olive oil. Bake at 175°C for 30 minutes. Serves 6.

8

9

10

11

12

13

14

15

There are at least five reasons to mulch: to keep moisture in the ground and so cut down on the watering; to prevent the ground from freezing too deeply (I do this with *Galtonia candicans*, the Summer Hyacinth or Spire Lily, which otherwise would not survive the winter in our zone); to keep the frost *in* the ground, so that the ground does not heave during warm spells and break plants' roots (this is particularly important if you have water-retentive soils); to keep down the weeds; and for aesthetic purposes.

You can use straw, shredded leaves, wood chippings, peat moss, pine needles, cocoa-bean shells (if you like the smell of chocolate) or even black plastic. Some mulches will remove nutrients from the soil, and you will need to compensate. Peat moss will form a crust and deflect water, and all mulches, if they are effective at blocking out the weeds, will also be effective at preventing the ''volunteer'' seedlings that are such an interesting element in a mature garden. But if you grow many plants of different kinds, the mulch may have a unifying visual impact upon the garden. Rock gardeners, for example, frequently use gravel, because alpine plants typically dislike moisture around their necks, but also because the gravel goes some way to offset the spottiness created by having many different individual plants.

16

17

18

19

Black Tupelo (*Nyssa sylvatica*).

PAMELA HARPER

20

21

22

23

Thanksgiving without pumpkins would be like Christmas without mistletoe. Pumpkins can not only be carved and lit so as to set a cold night aflicker with happy spirits, but can be used in the kitchen.

Pumpkin Soup

6 slices of crisp bacon, chopped, keep the fat
60 mL unsalted butter
1500 mL of peeled, chopped-up pumpkin
1500 mL of chicken or beef stock
125 mL Marsala, port or sweet sherry
chives, basil, thyme, salt and pepper
toasted pumpkin seeds

Heat the butter and bacon fat in a heavy pot. Add the pumpkin, and cook over medium heat, stirring occasionally, for 15 minutes. Add the stock, turn down the heat, and simmer until the pumpkin is soft (about 30 minutes). Remove from the heat, and add the wine, the herbs to taste, and salt and pepper. Pass through the blender to make the soup smooth, and simmer in the pot for a few more minutes with the bacon. Garnish with the pumpkin seeds. If you are feeling energetic, you could slice the top from a firm pumpkin, about a quarter of the way down, scrape out the pulp and pour in the soup! Serves 6.

24

25

26

27

Among the trees that provide fall color are the Sweet Gum (*Liquidambar styraciflua*, Z5) with electrifying crimson coloring; the Black Tupelo (*Nyssa sylvatica*, Z4), with orange, scarlet and yellow leaves; any of the Stewartias, with rich fall color of purple to orange, some hardy to Zone 5; the Katsura tree (*Cercidiphyllum japonicum*, Z4), with yellow to orange foliage; almost any oak, mountain ash and Japanese maple ('Osakazuki' is one of the most brilliantly colored); and I include one conifer, the Golden Larch (*Pseudolarix amabilis*, Z5), its name descriptive of its fall foliage.

Shrubs with good fall color include many types of *Viburnum*, some hardy to Zone 3 or even Zone 2; *Fothergilla* (Z5), with fine orange-red foliage, but requiring lime-free soil; the native Virginia Rose (*Rosa virginiana*, Z3); the Oak-leaved hydrangea (*Hydrangea quercifolia*, Z5) with dark-red wine colors; Winterberry (*Ilex verticillata*, Z3), which prefers an acid soil; and the Winged Euonymus (*Euonymus alata*, Z3), which is sometimes still in brilliant leaf when the first snow falls.

28

29

30

31

First snow on a Winged Spindle tree (*Euonymus alata*).

Royal Botanical Gardens/ Les jardins botaniques royaux

Spread over more than 1000 hectares along Highway 2, the Royal Botanical Gardens offer a diversity of habitat and garden display to satisfy any horticultural gourmet. The climate is mild by Ontario standards, permitting the vigorous growth of flowering and Japanese dogwoods and of the Japanese Hydrangea vine (*Schizophragma hydrangeoides*). Fall color is impressive, and the addition of the Mediterranean House has made the gardens a place to visit year-round.

There are five major areas, beginning at the central administration building, to which are attached conference rooms, displays of indoor plants, a courtyard, raised beds for alpines, and the spectacular Mediterranean House. Here, especially in the early months of the year, the thwarted gardener can roam among mimosas and eucalyptus, citrus trees and figs and olives, among colors and fragrances that recall happy holidays on the Côte d'Azur or in Southern California.

A short walk through some formal gardens with water, under the highway, takes us to the Rose Garden with its extensive selection of roses old and new, and to one of my favorite spots, the Harvey Clematis Collection, where species clematis, sometimes with unusually shaped flowers and unexpected leaf-forms, but all of great beauty, can be found in abundance. Nearby, arranged along a pergola, there are other climbers, including roses, wisterias, actinidias, and that best form of Trumpet vine, *Campsis* × *tagliabuana* 'Madame Galen'. Fragrant and Medicinal Gardens and the Trial Gardens for Annual Plants complete this complex.

From the Rose Garden, we walk west, once more crossing the highway, to the Laking Garden, famous for its iris display in early June and its thoughtfully planted perennials throughout most of the summer.

Some quick refreshments at the Rock Garden Restaurant, and then we continue on to one of the most famous parts of the Gardens, the Lilac Dell, where 1000 bushes make up the world's largest collection of species, hybrids and cultivars. This is a wonderful place to picnic at the end of May. The Teaching Garden includes a Herb Garden, and, finally, we come to the aptly named Cootes Paradise, an open shallow marsh around which are 40 kilometres of walking trails through geological and botanical diversity.

Royal Botanical Gardens/Les jardins botaniques royaux
P.O. Box 399
Hamilton, ON
L8N 3H8
(416) 527-1128
Outdoor gardens open daily from dawn until dusk. Mediterranean Garden open daily from 9:00 a.m. to 5:00 p.m.

The famed Lilac Dell.

November

The smaller your garden, the more important it is to exploit the vertical dimension. The range of climbing plants is wide. We all know roses, clematis, wisteria; here are some others: *Actinidia kolomikta* (Z4), with colorful variegated foliage; Five-leaf Akebia (*Akebia quinata*, Z4), a vigorous grower with small fragrant red-purple flowers in May; Trumpet Vine (*Campsis radicans*, Z4), with orange-scarlet trumpets in mid- and late-summer; Cup-and-Saucer Vine (*Cobaea scandens*, Z9), easily grown as an annual, and particularly beautiful in its white form; Chilean Gloryflower (*Eccremocarpus scaber*, Z8), but in colder zones can be used as an annual or as a perennial if grown against the side of a heated house or given considerable winter protection) with many small but attractive flowers in red, orange, yellow; Common White Jasmine (*Jasminum officinale*, Z7), with its famously fragrant white flowers throughout the summer; Red Chile-Bells (*Lapageria rosea*), with fabulously beautiful 10 cm red flowers during the summer, but very tender (Z10 or greenhouse); climbing honeysuckles (*Lonicera*) in all their variety, many hardy to Zone 4 or 5; exotic passionflowers (*Passiflora*, some species hardy to Zone 7); and another summer-flowering annual, Purple Bells (*Rhodochiton atrosanguineum*).

1

2

3

4

5

6

7

PAMELA HARPER

Lamium maculatum 'Beacon Silver'.

If you are thinking about constructing a new bed, you must think about its site, its size (especially in relation to depth), whether it is to be set against a wall or hedge in traditional fashion, whether it is to be "floating" (but anchored somewhere) or whether it is to be an island. The traditional bed sharply limits the number of positions from which it can be viewed, and, by affecting the way in which light reaches the plants, changes the pace and shape of their growth.

Whatever kind of bed you choose, whether it be free-floating or tied to a permanent feature, you still have to decide between straight edges and more sinuous forms. The choice is important, for shapes produce quite different experiences in the viewer. The straight lines are candid, tranquil, reasonable; the curves puzzling, concealing, disquieting, enticing, romantic. Perhaps the ideal garden has both.

8

The first dusting of snow on the garden.

9

10

11

REMEMBRANCE DAY

12

13

14

15

Here is a great way to use some of those apples that you picked earlier.

Tarte Tatin

Enough pastry for a single-crust
    23 cm pie
45 mL butter
60 mL sugar
1.35 kg peeled, cored and sliced
    Golden Delicious apples

Make enough pastry (sweet short-crust pastry is the best) for a single-crust 23 cm pie. Roll up and chill in the refrigerator.

Spread butter over the bottom of a round mold, and sprinkle with caster sugar. Put the mold over low heat until the butter melts and the sugar starts to caramelize. Arrange apples on top of the sugar, keeping them tightly together. Cook over low heat for about 30 minutes until the apples are soft and the butter, sugar and apple juices are beginning to run. Leave to cool.

Heat the oven to 190°C. Roll out the pastry, spread over the apples, turning up any surplus to make a crust around the edge of the mold. Bake for 20 to 25 minutes. Leave to cool, and turn out upside down. Serves 6.

Ground Covers

Vinca minor, or periwinkle, thrives best in not-too-sunny spots, and produces blue flowers over glossy green foliage in spring. It will grow well around the dry base of a tree and, where the ground is not too dry, acts as a nice foil for daffodils. Japanese Spurge (*Pachysandra terminalis*) is, like *Vinca*, evergreen and is almost indestructible; if *Pachysandra* won't grow, bring in the asphalt truck. Anyone who has seen the great stands along our roadsides of the wild orange daylily (*Hemerocallis fulva*) will know that it brooks no competition. The Fleece-flower (*Polygonum affine*, Z3) also belongs to this Rambo group, growing unstoppably over a sunny bank, though its kindly-sounding kin, the Rose Carpet Knotweed (*P. vaccinifolium*, Z7), with small red flowers on a plant about 22 cm high, is less aggressive, and is recommended where it is hardy. These all look best with lots of space, so use them boldly.

16

17

18

19

20

21

22

23

Pinks (*Dianthus ssp.*) on a dry sunny bank.

The injunction by the English poet, John Clare, to ''Dig old man's beard from woodland hedge, To twine a summer shade'' would surely get him into trouble today. Old man's beard is the *Clematis vitalba* of English hedgerows, similar in its vigor to the North American *Clematis virginiana*, and both would grow quickly over a pergola ''to twine a summer shade.'' Since both can be grown easily from seed, there is no excuse for digging them in the wild unless their habitat is about to be destroyed.

24

25

In the rock garden: *Phlox brittonii,*
Narcissus bulbocodium **and** *Dryas*
octopetala minor.

26

27

28

29

30

When the Frost Is on the Punkin'

They's something kinda'
   harty-like about the atmusfere
When the heat of summer's over
   and the coolin' fall is here —
Of course we miss the flowers,
   and the blossums on the trees,
And the mumble of the hummin'-
   birds and buzzin' of the bees;
But that air's so appetizin'; and
   the landscape through the haze
Of a crisp and sunny morning of
   the airly autumn days
Is a pictur' that no painter has the
   colorin' to mock —
When the frost is on the punkin'
   and the fodder's in the shock.

JAMES WHITCOMB RILEY
(1849–1916)

Small Deciduous Trees

If you have a good-sized property, then as a gift to your descendants you can plant a Wellingtonia or a Douglas Fir or a European Larch, all of which may, in good conditions, grow to 36 m in 100 years. If you have water, you can try a Swamp Cypress, with roughly equivalent results. Again, if you want to think really long term, you could plant an oak or two.

But most of us don't have a ''good-sized'' property. What we have is an urban or suburban lot in which we could comfortably plant one or two small trees (especially if we didn't have a great sugar or silver maple already taking up most of the garden). So here is a brief list of some small trees that I think are worth finding space for, with the orthodox hardiness zone. But remember that if you can find the right spot, you can often do better than orthodoxy suggests.

The Japanese maples (*Acer palmatum*, Z5) are glorious for their fine foliage, fall color, and the fact that they will accept some shade. The Snakebark maples, so-called because of the striped bark, are strangely neglected. Moosewood (*A. pensylvanicum*, Z3) is perhaps too large, but *AA. capillipes* (Z5), *grosseri* (Z5), *rufinerve* (Z5), and *davidii* (Z6) all sound perfect — if only they could be found! The redbuds (*Cercis canadensis*, Z4; *C. siliquastrum*, Z6; *C. racemosa*, Z7) are frequently gaunt, but always beautiful.

Dogwoods can be grown almost everywhere in North America except in the hottest, coldest and driest areas. *Cornus florida*, in spite of its name, is hardy to Zone 4, as is the early, yellow-flowering *C. mas*, which needs a decisive hand to make it into a small tree rather than a large shrub. The Japanese dogwood (*C. kousa*, Z5) has white flowers, raspberry-like fruit, and good fall color. Good fall color is also a characteristic of most of the hawthorns. *Crataegus phaenopyrum* (Washington Thorn, Z4), Watts Hawthorn (Z5), and the Cockspur Thorn (*C. crus-galli*,

Eastern Redbud (*Cercis canadensis*).

Z3) are all excellent in flower and fruit as well; we made a rather depressing jelly from the fruit of the latter.

Almost all of the flowering crabs are attractive, though I have a special fondness for three of the species, *Malus floribunda* (Japanese crab), *hupehensis* (Tea Crab), and *tschonoskii*, all hardy to Zone 4, the last-named with brilliant fall color. But do not forget the Carolina Silverbell, the Golden Rain Tree, and *Sorbus* 'Joseph Rock'; are their names not attraction enough?

December

Golden Rain Tree (*Koelreuteria paniculata*).

PAMELA HARPER

"The weakness of statues in most gardens nowadays lies in the fact that their powers of suggestion are irrelevant to their site. They are attention getters without logic behind them. And without logic, the intelligence and with it the beauty of a garden can collapse."

DIANE SAVILLE,
GARDENS FOR SMALL COUNTRY HOUSES

1

2

3

4

5

6

7

It is difficult to offer sage advice about the use of statuary in gardens.

We have placed a figure — angel, cherub, androgynous in any case — at the center of a small border. The border is backed by a hemlock hedge. The figure rests against the pleached wands of the Mayday tree (*Prunus padus commutata*), kept to 180 cm, and is surrounded by peonies. When the bed is at its peak, this small figure constitutes a ''still point in a turning world.'' It offers repose in the midst of a tumult of color and movement. And then, when most of the color is gone, it holds the bed together, its calm invitation deflecting our gaze from the subdued nature of the border. It is important that the figure not be maudlin. A perennial bed is romantic in its very conception, and its romantic nature needs a classical counterweight, not under-lining. The line is fine.

Northern gardeners are increasingly recognizing that winter is not a season totally lost, that a garden with good structure and careful planting will have its own shivery perfection. When leaves and flowers are gone, bark becomes more important. Here are some trees and shrubs that have attractive bark: many maples, but particularly the Paperbark Maple (*Acer griseum*, Z5), the Snakebark maples (*AA. capillipes*, Z5; *davidii*, Z6; *grosseri*, Z5; *pensylvanicum*, Z3; and *rufinerve*, Z5) and a Japanese maple (*Acer palmatum* 'Sango kaku' = 'Senkaki', Z5) with young branches of coral red; Speckled alder (*Alnus incana*, Z2) in its form 'Aurea' with yellow shoots and red-shaded catkins; the Strawberry-tree (*Arbutus*, Z7–8) with red-brown branches and peeling bark; the Chinese paper birch (*Betula albosinensis*, Z5) with pink and red peeling bark, or its form *septentrionalis*, which has orange-brown bark; the shrubby dogwoods with bright-red (*Cornus alba*, Z2) or bright-green (*C. stolonifera* 'Flaviramea', Z2) stems — use them together; the Snow Gum (*Eucalyptus niphophila*, Z8–9), which has bark of gray, green and cream patchwork; *Kerria japonica* (Z4) with canes of bright green, especially if thinned immediately after it has produced its yellow flowers; and many of the flowering cherries, especially *Prunus serrula* (Z5), with polished mahogany red-brown bark.

8

9

10

11

12

13

PAMELA HARPER

**Witch Hazel (*Hamamelis* ×
intermedia 'Jelena').**

14

15

Christmas lights in a black-and-
white landscape.

Winter

**Jim Woodford's
Grandmother's Carrot Pudding**

250 mL grated raw carrot

250 mL grated raw potato

250 mL grated and peeled apple

250 mL brown sugar

180 mL all-purpose flour

5 mL salt

5 mL baking soda

5 mL cinnamon

2.5 mL nutmeg

2.5 mL allspice

180 mL finely chopped suet

250 mL breadcrumbs

250 mL raisins

250 mL currants

Grease a 1500 mL mold. Combine carrot, potato and apple. Add brown sugar, and mix well. Sift together all-purpose flour, salt, baking soda, cinnamon, nutmeg and allspice, and add suet, breadcrumbs, raisins and currants. Toss with hands (though not if you've come directly from the garden) to mix well. Add the carrot mixture, blend well and spoon into the prepared mold. Cover tightly with foil, and set on a rack in a pan of boiling water (the water should come halfway up the side of the mold). Cover the pan tightly, and steam for 3 to 3 1/2 hours. Serve hot with a lemon sauce.

16

17

18

19

20

21

WINTER SOLSTICE

Clematis virginiana and **Clematis viticella 'Royal Velours'**.

22

23

Here are some plants that offer the *possibility* of flower in zones 8, 7, and exceptionally 6 — and even 5 between November and March.

The Higan Cherry (*Prunus subhirtella* 'Autumnalis') will flower with single, pale pink blossoms in Zone 7 from November to March. The Japanese apricot (*Prunus mume*) produces its pale pink flowers in early May in Zone 6, but also flowers in midwinter in warmer areas. It has a white form. The Chinese or David peach (*Prunus davidiana*) is said to be hardy to Zone 3, and produces its pink flowers in late March, or in January or February in warmer zones.

The choice of shrubs is wider. The wintersweet's (*Chimonanthus praecox*) "naked branches drip with waxy lanterns (of pale yellow) from December to March" in Zone 7. Winter Jasmine (*Jasminum nudiflorum*) is hardy to Zone 5, where it may flower in early April, but which will produce its bright yellow, scentless flowers for Christmas in gentler parts. Witch hazel has sweet-smelling yellow flowers (in *H. mollis*) and bronzy-orange flowers (*H. × intermedia* 'Jelena'). They prefer lime-free soil, and will sometimes flower in Zone 5 in February or March before the leaves appear. *Viburnum farreri* and *V. × bodnantense*, have fragrant white-tinged pink flowers in October and November.

24

25
CHRISTMAS DAY

26
BOXING DAY

27

28

29

30

31

PAMELA HARPER

Japanese Apricot (*Prunus mume*).

Seed Sources

Some of the best, and least expensive, sources of seed are the specialist plant societies. To obtain seed, you have to be a member, but membership brings other advantages, such as a regular bulletin, conferences and discounts on gardening books. Usually the societies have a seed exchange, which sounds intimidating to most of us, as we wonder what it is that we could send in that anyone else would want. But there is no need to worry, since you can ordinarily *receive* seed without being a donor. The advantage of being a donor is that you get first choice of the seed that other gardeners contribute, so you will soon be encouraged to start collecting seed from your own garden. Some of the specialist societies are:

Alpine Garden Club of
  British Columbia
Box 5161 — MPO
Vancouver, BC
V6B 4B2

Ontario Rock Garden
  Society
Box 146
Shelburne, ON
L0N 1S0

Cyclamen Society
Dr. D.V. Bent
9 Tudor Drive
Otford, Seven Oaks
Kent TN17 4LB
England

Rhododendron Society of
  Canada
R. Dickhout
5200 Timothy Crescent
Niagara Falls, ON
L2E 5G3

Alpine Garden Society
Secretary
Lye End Link
St. John's, Woking
Surrey GU21 1SW
England

Canadian Rose Society
686 Pharmacy Avenue
Scarborough, ON
M1L 3H8

The Canadian Wildflower
  Society
75 Ternhill Crescent
North York, ON
M3C 2E4

Hardy Plant Society
Conni Hanni
33530 S.E. Bluff Road
Boring, OR
97009

Clematis 'Voluceau'.

American Rock Garden
  Society
Secretary, ARGS
PO Box 200483
Denver, CO
80220-0483

The Heritage Seed Program
R.R. 3
Uxbridge, ON
L0C 1K0

Canadian Iris Society
342E 19th Street
Hamilton, ON
L9A 4S8

Herb Society of America
(Southern Ontario Unit)
Nordland Farms
R.R.1
Gormley, ON
L0H 1G0

These addresses change with some frequency, but letters will likely be forwarded. There are, of course, many good commercial suppliers, far too many for any comprehensive listing. Here are a few well-known, and usually dependable sources:

Dominion Seed House
Georgetown, ON
L7G 4A2

Gaze Seed Co.
9 Buchanan Street
St. John's, NF
A1C 5K8

Sanctuary Seeds
2388 West 4th Avenue
Vancouver, BC
V6K 1P1

Harris Seeds
3670 Buffalo Road
Rochester, NY
14624

Far North Gardens
16785 Harrison Street
Livonia, MI
48154

Thompson and Morgan
PO Box 1308
Jackson, NJ
08527

The Butchart Gardens
Box 4010, Station A
Victoria, BC
V8X 3X4

Stokes Seeds Ltd.
Box 10, 39 James Street
St. Catharines, ON
L2R 6R6

Park Seed
Cokesbury Road
Greenwood, SC
29647

W. Atlee Burpee
2544 Burpee Building
Warminster, PA
18974

Chiltern Seeds
Bortree Stile
Ulverston
Cumbria LA12 7PB
England

Gardening Records

Date	Jobs done	Jobs that should have been done

Date	Jobs done	Jobs that should have been done

Date	Jobs done	Jobs that should have been done

Date	Jobs done	Jobs that should have been done

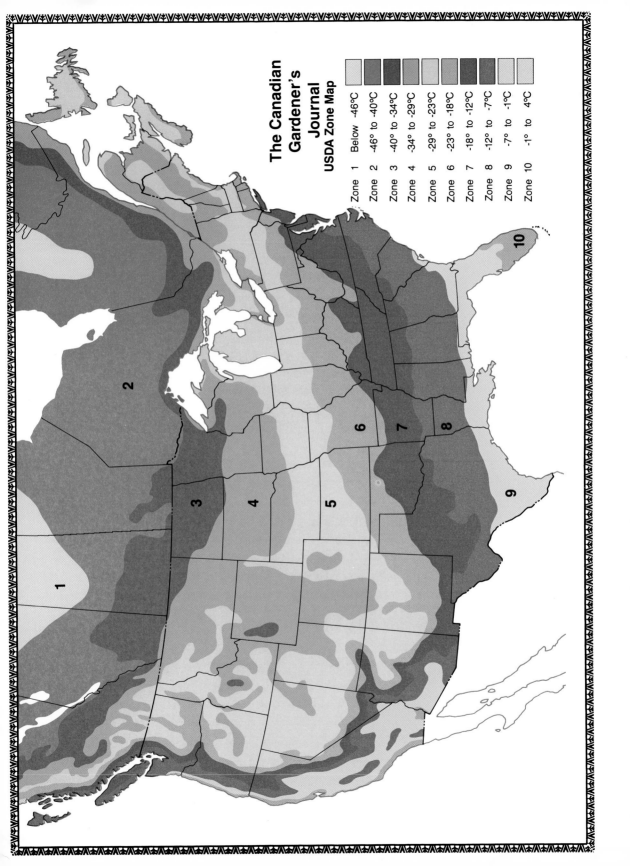

The Canadian Gardener's Journal
USDA Zone Map

Zone 1   Below -46°C
Zone 2   -46° to -40°C
Zone 3   -40° to -34°C
Zone 4   -34° to -29°C
Zone 5   -29° to -23°C
Zone 6   -23° to -18°C
Zone 7   -18° to -12°C
Zone 8   -12° to -7°C
Zone 9   -7° to -1°C
Zone 10   -1° to 4°C

Readings

The standard reference works, which should be available in your local library, are *Hortus Third* (Macmillan, 1976) and *The New York Botanical Garden Illustrated Encyclopedia of Horticulture* (Thomas, Everett, Garland, 1981). I continue to use Donald Wyman's *Wyman's Gardening Encyclopedia* (Macmillan, 1971). Trevor Coles's compilation of all the shrubby plants and trees carried by Canadian nurseries is invaluable (*Wood Plant Source List*, 4th edition, Agriculture Canada, 1987), and I find A.K. Buckley's *Trees and Shrubs of the Dominion Arboretum* (Agriculture Canada, 1980) extremely useful.

Mark Cullen's recent *A Greener Thumb* (Viking, 1990) has a lighter touch than most, and Marjorie Harris's *The Canadian Gardener* is written with verve and has beautiful photographs by Tim Saunders, but I still have a fondness for Lois Wilson's older *Chatelaine Gardening Guide* (Maclean-Hunter, 1970). First-class writing that goes beyond the white-fly-and-marigolds level comes from Allen Paterson in *Plants for Shade and Woodland* (Fitzhenry and Whiteside, 1987 — wittily written, woefully edited) and from Helen Skinner whose regular contributions to *Century Home* magazine cry out to be collected.

Gardening magazines include *Canadian Gardening*, *TLC*, *Wildflower* and *Harrowsmith*. Rock and alpine gardeners are often enthusiastic about a wide range of gardening, and the *Bulletin of the Alpine Garden Society of British Columbia* and the *Journal of the Ontario Rock Garden Society* should be attractive to the keen gardener.

A number of recent American books should be both useful and inspiring. They include *Perennials for American Gardens* by Ruth Clausen and Nicholas Ekstrom (Random House, 1989), *The American Weekend Garden* by Patricia Thorpe (Random House, 1988), Elisabeth Sheldon's *A Proper Garden* (Stackpole Books, 1989), Geoffrey Charlesworth's *The Opinionated Gardener* (David Godine, 1988).

Anyone interested in growing plants from seed will find *Park's Success with Seeds* (Ann Reilly, Park Seed Company, 1978) and the *Seedlist Handbook* (Mabel G. Harkness and Deborah d'Angelo, Timber Press, 1986) essential. For vegetable enthusiasts, *The Complete Vegetable Gardener's Sourcebook*, by Duane and Karen Newcomb (Prentice Hall, revised edition, 1989), is invaluable.